Of Love and War

OF LOVE AND WAR

A Collection of Poems By

JACOB PAUL PATCHEN

Adelaide Books
New York / Lisbon

2018

Of Love and War
A Collection of Poems
By Jacob Paul Patchen

Copyright © 2018 By Jacob Paul Patchen

Published by Adelaide Books, New York / Lisbon

Cover design & interior formatting:
Adelaide Books DBA, New York

Editor-in-Chief
Stevan V. Nikolic

All rights reserved. No part of this book may be reproduced in any manner whatsoever without written permission from the author except in the case of brief quotations embodied in critical articles and reviews.

For any information, please contact Adelaide Books
at info@adelaidebooks.org
or write to
Adelaide Books
244 Fifth Avenue, Suite D27
New York, NY, 10001

ISBN13: 978-1-949180-05-3
ISBN10: 1-949180-05-0

Printed in the United States of America

Dedicated to the war fighters, their families, and all of those forever altered by Operation Iraqi Freedom.

For the Marines and Sailors of 3/25 who shared their blood, sweat, and tears during that 2005 deployment.

For:
Cpl William Richardson
Cpl "Joey" Tremblay
SSgt Joseph Goodrich
LCpl Ryan Kovacicek

And for the brave 48 who gave their lives so that we could live ours.

Contents

PART ONE: FIGHTING

Rockets like You *13*

Love, My Sword *15*

Mortar Us *16*

Non-Alcoholic Beer *19*

Daddy's Tears *21*

Fireflies on the City *23*

I'd Love to Lay You Down *24*

Boys with Guns *25*

We Sleep with Mice and Vipers *28*

Throwing Rocks at the Shitter and Me *29*

Point Man *31*

Lime Trees in Paradise *32*

Unshakable She *34*

Gunshots in the City *35*

The Notebook and the Good Book *37*

Dog Barking at 4 a.m. on a Wednesday Morning *39*

Post-Traumatic Stress Disorder *40*

The Pistol on My Nightstand *42*

PART TWO: DYING

- *47*   Pieces of Depression
- *49*   To Feel Alive
- *50*   Death Letter
- *52*   The Wait
- *54*   Iraq, April 26th, 2005
- *56*   Dying in the Light
- *57*   Of Love and War
- *60*   Gone
- *61*   Cold Days without You
- *62*   Shadows in the Lamplight
- *63*   The Whore on my Left
- *64*   Humanity
- *65*   Dying at Work
- *67*   Living out Loud
- *68*   Grandpa Dying
- *69*   The Consolation Prize

PART THREE: REMEMBERING

- *73*   Where We Come From
- *76*   How You Catch Me
- *77*   To be the Westward Sky at Sunset

Hole in the Wall Woman   *78*

The Habits of a Broken Man   *79*

Are We Not Poets   *80*

On Seeing the Ginger from across the Bar
             and Hoping that She's Easy   *81*

Broken   *82*

Who I Thought I Was   *83*

Giving up, Giving Out   *85*

The Last Storm   *87*

How to Hold Your Head Up   *88*

Letting Go   *89*

PART FOUR: LIVING

How Alive Are We   *93*

Beer with Grandpa   *94*

How to Write a Poem   *96*

Drunk Heartedly   *98*

Tequila by Ten   *99*

Quake   *100*

Fall   *101*

This isn't About You   *102*

Aspiring Writer   *104*

105 Autumn in Her Arms
106 Sweet Red
108 Mixed Signals and Mixed Drinks
110 Tinder Me
112 Shopping Wal-Mart
114 Warm by the Moonlight
115 She Curses in the Morning
116 Dessert
117 Winter Coming
118 I Still Sleep with This Gun

121 ABOUT THE AUTHOR
123 ACKNOWLEDGMENTS

Part One

FIGHTING

OF LOVE AND WAR

Rockets like You

How strange a sound
        ripping through
this "love songs to think about me"

mixed-tape cd,
that you scribbled half shaded hearts
        and I love you's upon,
before you sent it out to this desert death land;

a sound roaring to life from afar   and dreamy,
        dragging jumping Marines
from their lover's arms
                to this concrete floor
of filth   and care packages.

Their presence is shaking.
And I have to watch the freeing grit
rush out   like South Carolina waves
        through the sun rays
gushing in from the sandbagged windows
            just to know that I am still alive.

Just as alive as I was with you
        while pretending to be a shark
           grabbing at your ankles
        in the salty tidal pools
of a past summer's vacation.

Jacob Paul Patchen

Now, the air raid siren sounds,
blasting validity through the barracks
    of sober faces.

It should have been a warning   well received,
about the woman   that you would become;

of how you would make that rumble
in the yard   become the roar inside of me;

how your uncertainty   and unfaithfulness,
    your fire and your shrapnel
left me charred and dying
        in a world of new beginnings.

Love, My Sword

I've yet to discover a blade
as sharp as Love.

A mighty sword in battle,
slicing down my enemies.

And, yet, such a fine,
shining steel to fall upon.

Jacob Paul Patchen

Mortar Us

I.

I can't see you from post three,
this dusty sandbagged bunker,
but I know you're out there. Hiding
behind your turban wrapped face;
you think you're a bandit; Ali Baba;
thief; stealing the peace from the night.

II.

The hum of my thermals sucking white
figures from the darkness tickles my nose
and drones out the river's wind. Though faint
and far away, I can still see the palms sway,
pointing towards the cities few speckled lights.
The green one, a mosque, flickers on and off;
there must be bombing up North. The power
cuts from the stone houses across the river,
normal, I know, but boredom hopes for more.

More buzzing down past the dunes, past
the groves, another boat spotlighting fish,
fishermen catching trout, or whatever the
native fish is.

It's been seven hours since the last explosion,
when evening prayer brought out the loyals.
And I'll never get used to those concussions,
but I've learned that the whistling means it'll
land over there.

I pick up the range card, which is permanently
marked on left over MRE cardboard. It's seven
hundred and fifty meters to the river. I click the
sights on my SAW to a thousand.

Stray dogs, matted, mangy, rabid
cousins of Brewskie back home, bark
at each other in a lust. It perks my eyes
to the East Ridge. It's all darkness now.
My NVG's can't penetrate the distance.
For a moment, I feel less of a killer;
vulnerable; blind. How did Hathcock do
it in the Jungle? I imagine that he slept with
Death, with the Devil, or some wicked charm
on fate. He must have been a smooth talker.
While here, I stutter on the radio.

III.

The thumps come in threes, sending red
headlamps running from the shitters. The
last one out, still holding to his trousers, is
swallowed up by the smoke. From this shelter,
I watch him die. Shrapnel to the throat, his
blood shinning scarlet in the Corpsman's
dim light. He couldn't even gargle his last words.

In sand and dust, you slither away; just like
that viper Phil found and let go at OP Paige;
you disappear into your oasis.

In sweat stained letters back home to dad,
I tell him and God how much killing you
would make me happy. I wait weeks for
restitution. But it never comes. Dad only
talks of home, and God only listens.

Non-Alcoholic Beer

I watched as the brighter desert cammies
carried in six wrinkled cases of O'Doul's
with the re-supply.

How ironic,
non-alcoholic beer for a bunch of soaked,
dry kids with guns.

Gunny says that it's to boost morale,
not looking up from his platoon counts
scribbled into a sweat-dried, camo-colored,
folding notebook pad.

"The limit's two."

His mundane was met with the typical
bullshit, deployment laughter, we hear
when things don't make sense.

How the fuck can they get non-alcoholic beer
into the city,
but not AA batteries for our NVG's?

I clench two warm cans and long stride it back
to my cot and the boys.

If beer is what it takes to be a man, then
let me pretend.

The first sip takes me back to Grandma's
basement card table, playing Old Mexico

until we threw up.

Daddy's Tears

1.

They didn't just stream down your face like mine.

While sitting next to you in that navy-blue sweater
Santa got me for Christmas, eight pews back from the Pastor,
I watched them build from the corners of your eyes.

It took them ten verses to wet your cheeks as you sat,
head bent, with your fingers and thumb at your brow,
shaking your knee up and down just like we'd play horsey
whenever you could find the time.

2.

I waited for the raised voices to stop before I tapped on your door.

As I sat next to your overnight bag on the bed, you told me
that we'd all be okay. And while you cleaned out your bedside
drawer, I asked if I could keep all the loose change and your
Old Timers folding pocket knife. Without pause, you placed them
in my little hands.

And from there, I watched them swell like those summer balloons
that we would wrap around the outside water spigot, and fill
until they burst.

3.

You stood next to mom for the first time in years.

Four white busses waited in a January's drizzle, shuttering
in the packed parking lot, buzzing with diesel exhaust, doors open,
soon sucking me into those cracked vinyl seats, my sweaty palms
sticking to them uncomfortably.

I was centered in my desert cammies telling you all that we'd be
okay. But as our last embraces were shared, from the bottom
of your throat they started, tickled up to your nose, and shivered
through your cheeks. But you held them in. You held them behind
bloodshot eyes and a cracking voice.

Instead, you told me that you would need my help next fall
tearing down the old Kroger's in town, and that I could run the roller,
compacting dirt for the new Sheetz coming in.

You told me that you love me.

And shaking my knee up and down with my head bend towards the
cold glass, my thumb and fingers firm at my brow, I counted blurry
mile markers, and thought back about that, as I bumped quietly
towards Cherry Point, North Carolina.

Fireflies on the City

Tracer rounds from helo's and grunts
on the ground arch through the air on fire.
Through my NVG's they look like fireflies
cast against the jagged backdrop of the distant
hills and city.

From this rear cliff, cutoff point, proned out
behind my gun in the dust – in ambush – I watch
the fireflies flicker down through the night.

They remind me of home when I was a boy;
shooting fireflies with water guns, watching them
burn through the backyard darkness and fade out.

I don't know why I did that. And I don't know
who I was back then.

Jacob Paul Patchen

I'd Love to Lay You Down

Lee Roy adjusts my slippery fingers
to the C chord on this scratched and
marked youth guitar that I asked mom
to ship from home five weeks ago.

I watch splashes of sweat, like mortars
inside the wire, burst at the frets as I
jerk awkward strums against these
out-of-tune strings.

I pull at my green and dirt colored sleeve,
wiping the sting from my eyes. It's been
over an hour, and we should be sleeping,
but the recent screaming rockets and thumps
of outgoing mortars still resonate in our
chests.

Lee Roy said that he would teach me.
And I promised to learn quickly. But these
short shaking fingers, slick with machinegun
oil and sweat, and longing for the goose-bumped
nape of your neck, fail to hold a tune.

I practice stretching them in my rack
as I mumble along with Conway Twitty,
fantasizing about October and our next
night together.

Boys with Guns

The *"bang-banging"* shot through the hills
like the cry of the stirred-up crow that we
didn't see until it was already circling above us.
And we were crows, hidden in the brush, high on
the hilltops – our perch – keeping watchful eye,
our beaks low in the foliage, at a whisper, our
attention at anything that moved, at any snap
or pop in the leaves and twigs.

We were hunters, predators, and scavengers.
We were snipers surviving the whining *"I got
you firsts!"*

Our camouflage didn't match. It was mostly
old scraps from Army/Navy stores and local flea
markets at the softball fields – all ripped, torn,
and with holes in the knees – but we didn't give a
shit. We were proud in our hand-me-down jungle
boots, with dirt smeared across our faces, and our
folding pocket knives, closed, and hidden, so that
Mother wouldn't see how much her boys wanted
to be men.

And, like men, we tried; crawling on our bellies
over moss and mushrooms, over acorns and shale
stones, dipping down into trickling creek beds, ready
to ambush, with water in our socks, waiting for the
perfect assault.

We thought we were men when wet feet and muddy
fists settled those arguments that words could not.

But even with blood dried noses and strawberried
elbows, we still ran like Rambo though the jungles
of Grandpa's twelve acres, screaming our battle cries,
and dodging imaginary bullets from plastic pistols and
tree limbed bazookas.

We were John Wayne and Clint Eastwood,
machine-gunning down our enemies up on top
of Heartbreak Ridge. We were pretending to
defend The Alamo.

The Alamo.

This Alamo.

Our Alamo.

Just some stone and mortar stuck out here in the desert,
with a bulldozed berm and razor wire around it.

It's not pretend, anymore.

Here, Al Anbar sand makes mud on my sweat ringed
combat boots, while we patrol in staggered columns
through the palms of the Euphrates.

And I think back to those days when we tried to be
men… and I wonder, now, if I am a man; or still
a child; or just stuck somewhere in between?

Now, this gun, slung tight around my neck, is heavier than I thought it would be. And it's loud. Louder than thoughts of home, or of crows and boys running wild through Grandpa's wooded hills.

These grenades in my pouch are real, they are cold, and they are taped down so that they do not explode in my face. They are nothing like those sticky pinecones that we used to throw.

And this steel blade beside them, zip-tied to the webbing of my flak jacket, is bigger than any of those old hardware store, display case, double bladed folders that I used to have. It's serrated, and has a blood groove for stabbing.

I keep it covered in pictures home for my mother.

Jacob Paul Patchen

We Sleep with Mice and Vipers

I live with a midnight eater. He scurries in
from the desert darkness, flashing tints of
moon from his sand shined fur. He's a Beast
in my bunker, ripping through granola bar
wrappers and the other half of my MRE crackers.
Soon, he will run for water.

There is no silence like that of the slant-eyed
hunter. He slithers up from the depths of Hell,
between sandbags, between sleeping bags,
between my rifle and me; He strikes midnight
eaters from the crumbs of my poppy seed pound
cake.

The ripping of wrappers has stopped.

I shift my machine gun to the front of me, adjust
my aired up and damp camping pillow, roll over,
and to the rumble of a snoring team and distant
helo's, I drift away to my backyard tent and home.

Throwing Rocks at the Shitter and Me

Hell. I can't even take a shit in peace.

Lee Roy's on over-watch, up the rocky hill
to my right, with his dirty machine gun
slung around his back, his Kevlar unstrapped
from a schoolboy's grin, chucking pieces of
the Promised Land down at me and the shitter.

The shitter. That's Funny.

Sitting on this jagged oval, hacked-out-
of-plywood seat, half fastened to a cut in half
rusted five-hundred-gallon drum --- probably
picked up from alongside Bronze, before it
could be made into a bomb just outside of the city.

Hey, it's better than digging a hole in ground --
I remember telling Justin when our three-days-late
re-supply dropped it off.

It's weathered, dirty, and has ashy shit paper spilling
from the vent holes in the sides. Lee Roy will mind
his boots, again, while he stirs the stench and flames
later this afternoon. For now, I hold still. The last
thing I need is a splinter or tetanus in my ass.

So here, I boldly sit, my pale ass in the dry morning wind, out in the open with the flies and the vipers and the occasional convoy passing by in a roaring cloud of dust and death.

My machine gun is as close to me as it can be, without laying doggishly across my lap (although, *here,* it *is* my best friend), as I stare out into this littered shithole that has become my home.

The dust devils are dancing against a heat waved scene of shit. The ground is shit. The hills and rocks are shit. My whole view is shit.

Hell, it even smells like shit, and sulfur, and sewage, and me, as I search out the distant shit hills, hoping that my desert cammies and this half-assed wadi keep me out of sight for self-instructed sniper fire.

Point Man

Brave threshold breaker, with
fast eyes and careful feet marking
fresh tread on fatal ground,

which we follow for safe
passage, one after another, with
heads on a swivel from freshly
patched walls to the peppered
rooftops and stench lined streets.

Or, when death screams from
shaded window and you are
called upon to advance, Brave
Threshold Breaker,
with a high firm pistol grip
and white knuckles griping

your M4 Carbine, pressed violently
into your shoulder;

we will follow thundering,
storming, raging our tide forward,
flooding bay to bay, downing
burning vessels. We will bring
the fall.

Jacob Paul Patchen

Lime Trees in Paradise

If I'm going to die, then let it be here,
in the shade of these swaying palms, under
this lime tree, surrounded by this garden's
green marble wall; *right here*, where we
took refuge from the sun and our gear.

A white stingered scorpion scurries across my
flak jacket laying in the dirt, dropped heavy, with
relief from slouching shoulders. If it's not the
bombs that will kill you, then it's everything else.

But, Sgt. Heller "*don't give a fuck!*" Neither do
I, anymore. So, I pick it back up and put it back on,
crashing back down to the Earth.

In this land, we are defeated by the sun. Swimming
in our cammies and hunched over by our gear, we go
firm behind these marbled walls to catch our wits.

Resting my gun on its bipods beside me, my
daggered back pressed up against this tree, I focus
on these fruits dangling and whipping in the warm,
burning wind.

OF LOVE AND WAR

I reach up into a blinding halo and grab the closest one, jerking it from its stem. And like an apple in Eden, without care or regret, and searching for the same kind of wisdom; I bite down into the rind; deep, full, and hard.

Smiling sweet, sucking victory, I relax; unpucker; and think back home, to my dad's salt-rimmed margaritas.

Unshakable She

She wasn't the hurricane,
or the loose and unfastened.

She wasn't the screaming wind
or the coming, ravenous waters.

She wasn't the squall.

She was the battered palm tree
that lasted.

OF LOVE AND WAR

Gunshots in the City

That's not where they're supposed to be.

Dad's stern voice stirs from the past and hits me
just as hard twelve years later, making me feel
like I've misbehaved again.

Back then, he left a homerun impression, smashing
my new Red Ryder BB gun against the oak tree in
the back yard; he convinced me that shooting
towards innocent people and houses was wrong.

And *here*, kneeling for cover in my desert cammies,
I still hesitate before I point my muzzle towards
an open window, where angry shots might have
come from just moments before.

But how are we to know what lies beyond that
dark, dark shadow?

A yawning baby in a swaddle? A room of bloody
faced women quietly condemning their ill-tempered
men who had no patience for their lack of haste
coming indoors when we passed by sweating and
smiling?

Is it children finding their father's rusty AK-47
underneath a stack of bright folded blankets, and
the oldest one, trying to impress Allah and his father,
points that shaking barrel out of his bedroom window
and squeezes down on the death trigger, going deaf
and dumb at the first shot?

The truth is, we don't know. How could we
in a place like this? A world of windows, walls,
alleys, and rooftops; one sniper could end us all;
and one child could send his family flaming to Hell.

OF LOVE AND WAR

The Notebook and the Good Book

I keep them together, in the top zippered flap
of my digital camo rucksack –
                    woodland green
in a place of shit brown.

I guess,
        we all should've seen
what we were up against from the start of it.

In between patrols,
        and in the few minutes before I collapse
into a new stain of old sweat,
I un-zip that easy-to-get-to pouch,
        pull out whichever comes first,
and recharge my wavering heart.

The Notebook   or the Good Book.
It doesn't matter at this point.

Each with worn, dog-eared pages,
        smeared with sweat
                and young men's dirty fingers.
We pass them around like that topless photo
of Lance Corporal Graham's
                cheating-whore-ex-lover.
I guess,
        Marines will always make a fickle girl famous.

But, there's no shame in crying hard
        about the things we cannot change,
when you sleep with a rifle tucked tightly and cold
beside you in your rack.

Where I keep this chipped-bladed k-bar underneath
of my dirty Cabela's camping pillow.

        Although, it is dull from knife
throws at sandbags, it still comforts
my shaking hand.

Because,
                the demons
that I fight
in my sleep   are mighty.

Dog Barking at 4 a.m. on a Wednesday Morning

What stirs us from these warm shallows
where daily thoughts and worries trickle
into visions of melting faces and debt-be-
gone solutions?

*Intruder? Cat burglar? Here to steal away
the cat hair and still lingering smell of cat
piss left on this football armchair, from a
time when I couldn't tell Kirstin no?*

No. This house is silent of cat burglars and
thieves out to meet their rapture. But Keela's
muffled, halfhearted calls into the night do
not fall upon deaf ears.

*Does she know that I'm awake? Would my
dog child even care? Would she nuzzle my
tired hand if I were to stumble out into the
darkness and ask 'what's the matter?'*

Perhaps she is having the same dreams as
me; free on the path that leads up through
the field where we walk for the view of
passing cars and ripe rolling hills. Free from
the debts of life, where slavery is an empty
dog dish and a sharp pile of unpaid bills.

Jacob Paul Patchen

Post-Traumatic Stress Disorder

It was obvious in that
still
jerk tight grip,

and that
still
wide eyed yank hard left
of that fresh sweat and ArmorAll
sticky steering wheel

that time
that I rattled my shining jeep
through a cold,
shallow mud
and dead leaf ditch

    still

    still

still searching backroad garbage for wires
and I.E.D.s
in the third week back home
from those shit and death streets.

It's right there in that
take cover jolt
and ready to swing clenching
of a rough shovel handle
      at the crack
of each tailgate **Boom**
from dad's old dirt and rust dump truck.

Or, on that whiff of black cloud exhaust
from a tired diesel engine
fast rolling those screeching tracks

      and I'd be back
      to up-gunning
      that machine gun
          again;

dark bandana over my breath
on a squinting, peppered face,
      scanning for the dead
in the sand and sulfur
of a death land.

And it's there just as obvious,
in my cousin's shock and awe face
while hunting for deer,
when I dropped
      to a raised gun knee
instincts aiming in
behind the cover of a fallen tree
as a camouflaged hunter's nearby shot

rallied up from the gully.

Jacob Paul Patchen

The Pistol on My Nightstand

I wake, fist clenched and damp.
The reflection of headlights, like flares
across my room, catch the fading words
of some lost sentence. Such a strange voice,
scared and mean; I haven't heard its tone
in years.

But now, eyes blinking and confused; there is
no sand, no sun, no warm wind stinging at my
cheeks. In the mixed glow of a quarter moon
and red alarm, I search the corners of my room.
But I see no threat, no danger; only a ceiling fan
buzzing low and sheets heavy, binding at my ankles.

To my left, mounted to the wall, my gun rack,
made of oak and cherry when I was a boy. The
different calibers make shadows like fingers
reaching out for me.

Under my mattress sticks a blade fixed to a
wooden handle. And at times I test its angle,
try its slicing steel; I feel for it before I sleep.

But on these nights, when thunder creeps in
from the West and shakes these walls, pulling
me from my past, I reach for the pistol on my
nightstand, feel its weight, its power, its comfort.

I pull the slide to the rear, let it go, hear the
clink of metal on brass and chamber a round.
I imagine the cavity in your chest; blood and
flesh burnt; pearl shards of bone; life smoking
from your holes; death; justice.

Then, barefoot and shirtless, I walk this house
armed until the morning sun.

Part Two

DYING

Pieces of Depression

There is something beautiful
        about falling apart.

This dirty linen, darkest on the pillow,
permanent in the middle and heavy;
    an ink blotch;
    a Rorschach test,
a self-evaluation each morning by ten.

If you ask me,

I see a shadow of a man with a burnt out
complexion, a smoldering disposition;

like those burnt crumbs still comfortable
        in last week's skillet
pushed to the back of a sticky stove;

like that familiar stench of old, rusty piss,
stagnate in this ring-stained toilet bowl.

        I see spots of toothpaste on this half-closed
bathroom window, where I stand, and I stare,
        and I listen,

waiting for inspiration, or direction,
        or for the world to end,
as I scrub at my chipped tooth and bleeding gums.

I see the *what-fors* and the *how-comes*
and the *why-nots*
    desperately interrogating
      these *who-am-I* eyes
in this hand-streaked, clouded mirror --- and broken.

Broken in the lower left corner, splintered
from the last time that I slammed it shut.

    Broken from this horned fiend reflection,
from worshipping this deity of misery,
from these crumbling thoughts

    of gun-muzzling this sickness,
of ending this agony.

But most of all,
broken from this monstrous conclusion:

    that I am <u>not</u> the hero that I need to be.

And shattered
into scarlet and grey pieces of depression.

To Feel Alive

No pistol tastes the same.

    Mine

is a bourbon muzzled truth maker;
as bitter

as those night terrors

of a columned world around me

    exploding;

as real as self-inflicted regret;

so familiar in my hand,
    and cold on my tongue;

It burns
    on the way down.

Jacob Paul Patchen

Death Letter

On this green, issued, sweat stained cot,

in salt-stiff desert cammies,

I drip words from my pores, like blood
from shrapnel wounds.

It   is hot. And thoughts of you steam
my blood.

To say goodbye to smiles in a pile of pictures

    is prison.

But, *here*, there are no visiting hours; no
holiday breaks to touch your skin.

I am captive in this foreign land;

a slave to a unit number;
                    a digit in a media war.
I am a piece of paper to a brass paper weight; filled
with training checkmarks, achievements, and
        next of kin.

No amount of wind will let me fly.

I am chained in this sand, blindfolded and bound,
as useful as a rotting corpse;
        without life… without soul.

And I am days away from that kind of death.

Or maybe minutes, or hours,
        or even the seconds that tic loudly by
on this olive drab, sun faded watch.

I'm writing to say goodbye,
              because, by now,
I have accepted it.

Jacob Paul Patchen

The Wait

I sit two empty chairs away from a chubby mother
whose blush is almost the color of her red curly hair.
Her kids are in the play room, quietly running the red,
blue and yellow beads up and down a matching
colored maze of rails. That toy never interested me.

The buzz of the dying bulbs overhead reminds me
of exam room three; they still haven't changed
that burnt out light. The pale, plain walls are near bare
and paper-white—meant to ease my mind, I'm sure.

Instead, I feel as empty and as numb as that photo
of maple and oak under a dusting of painted snow;
And I wonder why they would hang something
so dead in a place for the ill and dying.

My mother sits beside me in a faded, peach, zip-down
hoodie. She folds over yesterday's paper that she brought
from home and rereads the article on cancer survivors.

When I think of boredom, I think of us.
Five times in the last ten minutes she raised her slim
and silver JC Penney's watch to check the time.
I try counting goldfish in a tank that sits in the center
of the room, again, until my name, from an open side
door, raises the thin, dark hair on my arms.

OF LOVE AND WAR

When I walk through the door of exam room three,
that bulb still unchanged, the scent of sanitation
and medicine overpower the lingering last night's
lemon mopped floors. I left a waiting room to wait
in a room again.

The process, as familiar as sixth grade lunch,
I wait for it all morning, just to end up waiting again
in a line of hungry, noisy kids. I can tell it's getting
to be lunch time.

He enters with a knock, as if I would be at home
in a place like this, and lumbers in, white jacket flashing
with his long strides. It reads Dr. Charley Chabachnick,
a familiar name that I still can't say right, so I call him *Doc*.

His hands are rough and cold, as if he had been
in that waiting room for as long as we had. His breath
smells of garlic, making my stomach growl.

Pinning two MRI pictures to the bright lights on
the wall, he points to the center of a light blue and
black, illuminated head.

My head. My brain. My tumor.

"It's no longer growing." He says with an accent.
Mom thinks he's Slovak.

And we walk out holding hands, mother and I,
down the hall, into the elevator, and out the doors
to her bright jeep waiting in a burning sun.

She's taking me to Red Lobster.

Jacob Paul Patchen

Iraq, April 26th, 2005

Tears swell and drip like open wounds.
They fall wet, but dry before sandy streets
can taste their pain, when wind as warm
as Satan's breath carries each drop off into
the burning sun.

How many tears did it take to fill the Euphrates?
How much deeper must it go?

Shhh! The thunder of Death comes.
Blow by blow, rain from a cloudless sky explodes.

And again, gardens of fouled flesh bloom.

Or, up from the quaking ground, the Devil grabs
at our limbs, pulling us back into this earth.

"I never met his mother, but in my dreams
she wore my mother's face. Alone, bent
over needle and thread, rocking and sobbing,
sewing Joey and tears into the flag. Then,
we stand before her under an unforgiving sun,
lined in perfect ranks, saluting with perfection.
One by one she stiches what it means to be American
across our breast."

"I've never understood what it means, but I wake
up every time with a pain in my chest."

Again, the thunder of Death comes....

There's no Jesus left in this Fucking land!
Allah walks freely in streets lined with wired death!
One shot killers blend in a nation of covered faces.
Mercy – has fled – with the innocent!

On my cot, prayers are sent by mail, kisses on pictures.
I put home back under my rack. There's no room for
weakness in my blood today. I print JOEY onto brass
and let him ride the bolt into my chamber.

Today he patrols with us again. Today he is my trigger.
Today he will rest in peace.

Jacob Paul Patchen

Dying in the Light

The shadows here are tall and mean.

A darker version of myself, armed and just as dirty; stretching out towards home, or freedom, or forgiveness; only to fall short of that salvation.

A dark angel beside me, who looks like me, who moves like me, but is able to bend along these desert walls, hugging to the cover of concrete and marble, if it wants to;

or fearless, poking out into the open streets; daring poor bastards to fire, to expose their hidden intentions, to invite in that kind of death and destruction.

    My shadow is a cold-blooded warrior; faceless and stern. But in the heat of a flaring sun, he still catches me when I fall.

Of Love and War

I.
I don't remember the last time that we got mail,
or which stained cot or shithole that I was in
when I opened it

and read about your summer days sun bathing
in your new 4th of July two-piece out at the lake
with Eric and Tori. Or about how softly your
mother cried, lifting and dabbing behind her glasses
with a wadded-up tissue, while helping you pick
out new linens for your hour-and-a-half away
dorm room bed.

But now I sift through this pile of white and
mixed colored letters, moving my family's
and friend's aside, and stacking yours on top by
the date that you carefully wrote on the outside seal.
And, one dirty thumb print after another, I open
them all chapter by chapter.

"Jake, I love you."

"Jake, I love you."

"Jake, I love you."

I kiss them all, one by one, fading away into
winter thoughts of us and the last time that
we touched. And still visible splashes of your
perfume reminding me of your neck, when I would
press my tongue and lips against it, making
you bump up with chills, just as these thoughts
of you do to me now.

I lie down damp and hope for dreams of us,
like that summer before, on a fuzzy blanket in
the sharp grassed field beside my father's house,
where romance was slapping mosquitos from
each other's backs under partially cloudy stars
and stirrings in the woods beside us. We made it
quick, but lasting.

II.
"Seventeen days until I see you… until I touch
you, until I kiss you."

My voice quietly hiding the excitement in a
room full of hardened Marines murmuring
trying to hold back tears on phone calls home.

But your voice is not as I remember it from a
month ago. Your "I miss you's and I love you's"
sound shaky, barren, and empty. I pass it off as
nerves and swallow down a warm meal to fill
the pit in my stomach.

For the first time since nine months away, I fear
that I don't know you.

III.
I've laid restless for hours beside your steady,
easy breathing. And mine is sharp, shallow, and
forced from gritted teeth. Between you and the
ceiling, I can't stare anywhere else. The hugs
from earlier have worn off, and the kisses weren't
as warming as I had imagined.

Your bra is still fastened, your Levi's are
buttoned, and the long-sleeved shirt I offered
you to wear, is sitting on the chair beside us. You
are wearing what you wore to my brother's football
game, and I've spent hours trying to figure out why.

IV.
Eventually, tomorrow morning will come, though
sleep will not. And you will finally tell me about
Stephen, with a *phh,* from school.

And I will mock him, threaten to kill him, to gut him
with my K-bar knife,

to gouge out his eyeballs and skull fuck his corpse.

You will cry; and I will rage.

I will scream out in a voice that I thought I buried
just weeks ago, and it will scare me to the core.

You will shed believable tears down your flush
cheeks, and I will still want to hold you. I will still
want to love you; though, I can't.

Gone

standing barefoot
        in a muddy puddle
looking up

on a sunny summer's day

        trying to evaporate
right along with it

and you

Cold Days without You

The wind has turned against me;

a pink nose and rough lips
swaying along with the limbs,
whipping and crackling like our
last Summer's blaze flaring in
your eyes, lighting up the edge-
of-the-yard elms and me.

Without that warmth, your January
thoughts are shivers.

Shadows in the Lamplight

The night is nothing more than
bad imagery and perspective:

Beer bottles loom like tombstones,
marking where dead worries lie.

Their shadows lean crooked and
bent by the dim lamplight.

A heavy head to a dirty pillow on a
dog haired couch; what cares have I?

And if it wasn't so damned cliché, I'd
admit that she broke my humbled heart.

But in this moment of stale air and hatred,
the truth is easier to see; I broke it myself.

The Whore on my Left

Deep emerald eyes, as dark and
mysterious as last Spring's
backyard sink hole.

And I sink into them,
    swirling,
half swimming, half floating;
breaststrokes and
deep desperate breaths.

I am drenched in their misery.

Shirtless. Lifeless. Bare skin
half covered by ocean covers;
smeared and stained. Full of stench
and sex.

I hate it. I need it.

Where is the place for those who
get their pleasure from vessels of
sorrow?

I wonder as I stare into those green
and webbed eyes,

"How can you love like this?"

I mumble to the jaded reflection
to my weak side.

Humanity

How could you not see
that I was dying;

stumbling by with a
loaded bottle to my brain,

speaking to you in whispers,
about me in tongues,

dragging my anger behind
me like a dead dog on a leash?

I was tall when I was crawling,
but you stepped right over me

like a crack in the sidewalk.

Dying at Work

We're all dying in our work clothes.

Lying gray and lifeless on the floor
halfway into the break room; buttoned-
up dress shirt, threaded and stitched
together, holding in the stench of waste
and decay.

Zipped and buckled to be proper, I.D.
badge and nametag that reads JACOB,
so that they will know who once made
this suit move; who would walk back
and forth to the copier in these stiff penny
loafers, clicking this ballpoint pen, half
inkless from signature after signature,
signing away valued time in a place of
emptiness, of worthlessness.

To shed this shirt and run, to wrap this
red tie around my head like an office
Rambo, ducking in and out of cubicles
for cover,

a stapler as my weapon, fending off the
hours, the minutes, the angry moments
gone from you, from them, from us.

Jacob Paul Patchen

I will shimmy from these slacks and leave
them wadded up in my rolling cushioned
swivel chair, where they will feel at home.

I give these calf high socks to the filing
cabinet; these scuffless brown shoes to the
bathroom trashcan, where I would throw
away time alone.

And out into that fine, free air I will strut,
victorious, in my bright blue boxer briefs
and flashing red tie, free. Free. Freedom.

Living out Loud

Life–

how quiet
    we are
at a time
when disturbance

    is needed.

Jacob Paul Patchen

Grandpa Dying

I cannot hear the distance
in your voice,

but I can smell the rotten
on your breath.

Your eyes have gone milky,
red and blue.

It reminds me of the patriot
in you,

and I wonder

if you can still see in me
the ornery blonde screamer, tree
climber and fighter

that I used to be.

And I hope
that you think of the stubbornness
that you spent years teaching me,

even

as you hold onto

these last long breaths.

The Consolation Prize

How many breasts have been painted purple
at a time when purple means red and red is blood
and blood means sacrifice?

Too many can talk of sacrifice.
A story for each tear. Roadside bombs,
Rockets from the sky, Double-Stacked Mines....

The Purple Heart;
a blood-soaked medal to replace
your arm, your leg, your life.

"Congratulations marine, you've been injured."

"Thank you, Mr. President,
as soon as I learn to walk again, I'm going
straight home to place this up high on my mantle."

Part Three

REMEMBERING

OF LOVE AND WAR

Where We Come From

Mostly empty Old Milwaukee cans, stashed in the garage
behind the wd40 and lined quarts of oil,
clamor from this year's litter of curious Calico kittens.

And there's new, stubborn, Slovak blood
rolling down the old stains on Grandpa's smeared
and greasy knuckles.

But he just grunts like the buck at the backyard apple tree,
where he built cousin Ju-Ju's square plywood tree fort
that now gives shelter to a lost nerf football and a few
forgotten GI-JOE army men;

there was a time,
back before he had us grandkids searching faithfully
for "purple-assed-buzzards,"
that he would have cursed at the pain of a slipped wrench
on a buddy's rusted old Chevy,

back when the pain of hard labor could still make new scars,
like the blizzard of '77, when the water pipes froze solid
and he lumbered out into the wind and fury, both before
and after work, to stretch a garden hose across the driveway
in order for his little girls to take a cold shower.

Or, back when Grandma's open heart would carry in
another stray animal, or another friend without a place to go,
back when the guest bedroom was always full, and no mouth
would go unfed, unless it was hers or his;

A cursing time, but a blessing time;

when he taught little girls to how feed the horses, peacocks,
and chickens before school, so that they could run off to class
learning how to live with the shit on their shoes;

or how to get dirt and blisters on their hands,
shoveling out the chicken coop into five-gallon buckets
to fertilize the sweet peas and cabbage;

or plucking bloody feathers from a freshly axed hen for dinner,
and standing on a bucket at the sink in the garage
washing out the gizzards and thumbing off dried shit from
those brown speckled eggs with a grease bubbled bar of Lava soap.

The same eggs that were gathered on the ice or in the mud,
both morning and night. Then, sending them off in saved cartons
to church, neighbors, or school, to those who needed them more
than a house of half full stomachs.

"There is always someone who is less fortunate than you."

I remember Grandma would often remind us, while ignoring another
one of my temper tantrums on the floor of Kroger's candy aisle
as we filled church Christmas baskets; or, back then, when she had
to cash in her silver certificates in order to buy Pamra's new braces.

OF LOVE AND WAR

But now, here in the garage, Grandpa's new greasy bubbles,
on the same green bar of soap, turn my small, dirty-fingernailed hands
grey while I watch him wipe that still stubborn, Slovak blood dry
on Aunt Penny's new birthday flannel.

And the dogs are barking at mom walking across the hill,
while Grandma is sweeping leaves from the chairs and swing
on the patio, as more familiar faces sling gravel up the drive;

their hatches filled with homemade pie, pagachi, and corn on the cob
for the fire. The cousins are dressed too nicely in their collared shirts
and bright sneakers;

and later, we will be scolded for our creek-soaked shoes
and grass stained jeans, swinging at lightning bugs with sticks,
and bragging about sleeping in the tent all night,

but waking up, instead, at the foot of Grandpa's snoring bed
in Aunt Patti's old basketball sweats.

Jacob Paul Patchen

How You Catch Me

There wasn't an oak too high for me
to climb.

Jeremy, in his tiny, G. I. Joe t-shirt
and high-water jeans, double-dog-daring
me to try.

So up I would go, hugging tight to the bark
like my mother's leg in the candy aisle.

And Jason, with his spotlight hair and
bright sky eyes, would cry.

But it didn't stop me from feeling the
birds breeze by, or from getting a little closer
to Jesus,

as I would bend that branch back down,
my little ninja-turtle sweats and used-to-be-white,
mud-crusted sneakers, stretching and kicking,

lunging out towards emptiness,

only to feel the strength of four little hands,
my brothers' hands,
reach up and grab me, steady my crazy,
and guide my shaking legs back down to safety.

To be the Westward Sky at Sunset

I want to be
the westward sky
at sunset, when
blues melt and trickle,
drip into fire, burn red
and glow orange;

warming to the eyes,
like wool mittens
in Montana's winter,
when frost nipped
fingers go numb, tingle,
and turn pale white;

white as the sun streams
that break free from
the covering grey clouds,
when thunderheads build
over prairie-dog plains
and rocket through the sky
a web of busted dreams;

like when she twisted
this ring from her finger
and set it down on white paper,
as empty as the six syllables
that filled it:

"I have to find myself," it said.
And just as frankly, off she went
into the west fading sun.

Jacob Paul Patchen

Hole in the Wall Woman

I told myself that I wouldn't do this again.

Well, I lied.

To me, and to you. For saying that I didn't care.

And now, it's just me and this wall patch and scraper, these left-handed strokes of sandpaper.

We're nothing more than falling pixy dust in a fairytale,

and

I'm just making a mess on the floor.

The Habits of a Broken Man

Your words were hope laced poison.

And I drank them in like the fool that
I am; smiling; nodding; oblivious to
the evil inside of you. I cast out my
humbled dignity, and you sucked it,
and me, right in.

And since I'm confessing, I'll be
completely honest, had you not looked
so seductive in the beer light, I'd never
have said hello.

Give me a break. It had been five barren
months, and you were willing; all I had
to do was invite you in.

    But I awoke alone and ashamed
by morning's pointing light.

Jacob Paul Patchen

Are We Not Poets

Are we not poets;

those of us who drink our words in at the
Midnight hour, in the darkness of a crowded bar?

Loud, obnoxious friends, impressing No One.
No One will care, No One will comfort come
bitter morning, in the fog of who we used to be,
as we regurgitate our lines, one groaning flush
at a time,

like wadded scraps of paper in a wastepaper basket,
we watch our stupid words swirl, angry, down the
drain… and hopeless; just like in the hours before,

"Hey baby, did it hurt when you fell from Heaven.
God, must've spent a little more time on you."

Idiot… Poor. Misguided. Self-indulged Idiot;

whose dry heaves are like the dry fires in the mirror
last night, back before, when you practiced smiling
just right. But, no more smiling this morning, not
in the stinging of an opened blind limelight.

Because here, your words leave you empty, cold,
and uninspired.

On Seeing the Ginger from across the Bar and Hoping that She's Easy

We've all done it, those of us without
reserve. The ones hell bent on giving in,
giving up, giving out.

I give temptation its due, join the night time
prowlers slumped onto bar stools, packed
into corner booths, watching with glowing eyes,
with eyes for the cat.
        Chasers.

We run in packs like wild dogs,
        salivating at the scent of melon shampoo
and Love Kills Slowly perfume;

each one waiting for the herd to thin, for the strong
to drive off to their waiting lovers in waiting beds
with waiting comforters.

It's the wounded that are weak;
        the ones with limping hearts.

And we pick them off one by one. Buy them
a Lifesaver, an Orgasm, Sex on the Beach; tell them
we want them and then take them home.

There we sink our teeth and down our prey by the jugular;
watch them squirm, twitch, shutter, and stain our sheets.

By morning, there is nothing left.

Broken

One trumpet spills its melody from
open window to open window. The
rusty voice of air and reed forced
from the lips and lungs of a sorry
poet whose pen is brass n' shrill.

Oblivious musician knows no
audience, but my somber reflection
and half open window sit alone half
broken.

And I wonder, now, if she heard the
same busted chords and melody,
would she be thinking of me?

OF LOVE AND WAR

Who I Thought I Was

When I think back to who I thought I was,
I see myself in three-hour conversations
about nothing, or something, or anything,
just happy to pass the time.

I think back to making love to her;
no, not making love… fucking her,
love is what I called it to feel less guilt.
Love is the word that I used to make
my tired heart feel alive.

I was a romantic without romance.
I was a love song without lyrics,
an amplifier unplugged; useless.
I had a microphone with no power,
a book of words to say, but I
spoke a different language, she
wouldn't have understood anyway.

I was in love with love,
anyone with tits and a smile
would've done. Anyone willing
to let me talk, to empty my heart
(and that she did) would have pleased me.

Jacob Paul Patchen

But I can see now, or feel rather,
that who I thought I was, was simply
who I wanted to be.

Three hours we'd spend in conversation
each night, about what... I don't know.
But she let me tell her I love her,
and that's who I thought I was.

OF LOVE AND WAR

Giving up, Giving Out

She wasn't nearly as pure
after the breakup, whoring around
like those Facebook love affairs
that we would often shake our heads
about.

I tried to keep in touch, on drunk nights,
but I knew that she was gone, sucked into
the thrills of nonbelievers.

I hated her for that.

For giving up on the woman that she wanted
to become.

For fucking away the future
that we often talked about over a full glass
of blackberry wine, under those Autumn sparklers,
while rubbing her thigh and wishing for forever.

But forever always comes too soon.

We were young souls in aging bodies,
lost in the excitement of something new.

But we knew.

We knew that love was sour,
that life was quite bitter after the sugar coating.
But we kept sucking, anyway.

And now, that's how she forgets about me.

The Last Storm

I must have left you, then,
during the last storm,

dashing boldly for a better
shelter, hands up for cover,
splashing through your
torrents and rampage;

    because, quite frankly,
raindrops and hailstones are
not the same,

and your spring showers had
turned to ice.

Jacob Paul Patchen

How to Hold Your Head Up

Stop watching where your feet go.

Aimless steps into the shadows
of a burnt-out hallway light,
      too high to reach,
      too high to care,
tripping over angled hurdles placed there
by a careless moon; gilded
      in the darkness
      for the lost to find;
armored, and shinning for your curses
and flying stones.

Aim high when you're desperate.

Pot shots at the moon, at the sun,
both too bright for your dark thoughts.
Angry haymakers wild at a wall
      that is there
      to hold up
the shell that you are.
And now you swing holes into it,
      like a lunatic
      aiming to break,
you shatter.

Cold on the dark floor, you look up for help.

Letting Go

For fuck's sake gentle souls,
    breathe;
calm your dying hearts;
    let it be.
It is.
You are.
I am.
    Silence.
Stop wasting
your troubled thoughts
    on nonsense.
We are here to be,
so be.

Part Four

LIVING

How Alive Are We

How alive are we, the living?
The ones lakeside smiling; raised,
cold coozy, wet from a warming
Busch Light's condensation in the
8:45 fading of a summer's sky....

Red in the cheeks and sparkling,
damp neck collar from building
the fire blazing in the sinking
shadows, where later we will dip
for private consultations about
the moments where we feel most
beating.

"I'm alive!" You will scream, flashing
pale tints of sunburned tan lines as
you splash down into the moon-rippled
water, and me.

Jacob Paul Patchen

Beer with Grandpa

We stood like soldiers there in
the chill of November's morning,
guarding our feast with loaded cans
aiming to kill the boredom. I was still
shaking off the clouds of late night
rompings; you were just getting started.

But the Bud Lights went down like
the bottled water that Grandma said we
should've had, their nipping cans biting
at our fingers. I watched you pull out
the work gloves from both sides of your
flannel jacket, and I slid the camouflaged
coozy from my torn jeans' back pocket.
We both grinned with our preparedness.

Around us was your home, my playground;
twelve acres of woods and rolling hills, all
grey with the coming winter. In back, the
raspberry patch we nibble in mid-summer's
heat; where you had once laughed when I
unfolded the knife from my left hip pocket
and picked at the seeds in my teeth.

Down the hill stood the chicken coop we built. And when the wind blew South, we could smell your cherished brood. But there between us, the deep fryer was warm, fifty feet from your stained brown wrap around porch. The peanut oil bubbling, smoking, and blending with our breath; It smelled of fall, family and giving.

We talked of the days we both could remember; all our cars and trucks that you fixed, the chickens we plucked from the pines at night, the front porch coons you shot and the one that you missed (and stubbornly, you still say that I fouled up those sights of that old twenty-two, which now sits on the top notch of my built-it-myself gun rack).

Later, when we stand around a full table of bread, and I call on you and you call on me to give our grace. I will bow my head and listen as you thank Him for our food, family, and freedom, while I silently give thanks for you and this morning's company.

How to Write a Poem

I don't know how you do it,

but I tune it all out, sink into
the hum of outside crickets
and chirping tree frogs, forget
who I've become, or the far-off
places that I haven't been.

I get washed into dying memories
of childhood mud and crunching
fall leaves under hand-me-down
hunting boots; I feel them,
I become them.

I listen to the sound of my own
thinking, of my own drumming voice;
a steady rhythm in my head, sounding
out images of buzzards circling
the scarlet skin and snow-white bones
of a dead deer decaying in the woods;
my lips wet and moving, my tongue
flicking quiet words at a piece of paper
earning its stripes.

And out it flings in scribbles,
like vomit on the wall, sliding green
chunks of yesterday's youth and
mustard swirls of this morning's certainty.

Ugh, the smell of digested life.

I wipe my mouth clean on this faded,
college football cut-off, gargle
with cool pale coffee, and clean up
the mess.

    And then,
like the excited child that I am,
I interrupt your programming
for you to hear me.

Drunk Heartedly

The frantic light from one too many flames
flicks at your curves and cavities making it clear
not to keep any secrets. Instead, we share
ourselves completely, entirely, until we collapse,
bare breasted on damp sheets.

Some time goes by before you move.
And I know now that you are not dead, nor asleep
from exhaustion.
And I too move, searching for my breath
in the warm air of sex and dirty clothes piled high
in the corner.

I let out a breathy moan, more for me than you,
if not only to hear that I am alive, that I, in fact,
do exist. And that *I am* here, right here, in this
moment of love and satisfaction.

But now, I am drained, and with cramping thighs,
and bulging arms, I drag myself back from this
fantasy to reality. I slide from these tangled sheets
to the littered floor. I steady myself on the bed,
on my writing chair, on the wall; and I stumble,
and I waddle, drunk heartedly
        into the darkness of the bathroom.

Tequila by Ten

It's no surprise that we didn't
bother getting dressed;

we are more alive when we are
        uncovered.
And how wild we are drunk dancing
to the rhythm of deep laughter.

Your bare breasts tango in the
morning light.
I simply cannot get enough of
the woman that you are.

        Body shots of a tequila
sunrise;
        and in my eyes, you are
        everything.

Quake

I was shaken and unstable.
And you were a California
Redwood, pointing up as
I was coming down.

I was a blind leaf weaving
in the Autumn wind. And
you were rooted; solid; a
part of the ground.

You did not flinch when your
soft fingers caught me. And
I did not fear the quake of two
bodies crashing into one.

Fall

Your coming brings the red leaves.

They sweep across my face like
strands of Autumn hair when you
lean down to kiss me.

I watch the fields for erotic antlers.

Their swaggered steps, so deliberate,
so passionate, so slow; like when you
take charge of making love to me.

We kiss in the fever of a campfire.

Its rusty flames, back and forth, giving
and taking, tangled like hands, like faces;
like us in the wild of an October's night.

Jacob Paul Patchen

This isn't About You

I write for me, but to read to you…
and then judge you for judging me.

I write to taste life; language; to hold
these words between tongue and cheek,
sucking out the bitter juices of gnarled up
vocabulary.

I write for attention; my attention, as it so
often drifts toward you.

But I pull it back with run-on-sentences
about undressing you with my eyes and then
my hands and then touching you with my
finger tips because I want you and I want to
be with you because I need you because you
are everything to me.

And there it goes, off again, to the curves
and refractions of your pale ass flexing in
the door-opened-hallway-light.

But this isn't about you… not yet.

OF LOVE AND WAR

I write for me. It's the *"I"* in this stanza that
stands out. Like a river in the desert, or palms
giving shade to those in Hell, I walk the dirt
roads back to my childhood. Back when trees
were giants that I would sling-shot to the top;
back when mud and sticks and bark made forts
for the day. I played army, but never died
because I knew magic.

And now, out loud, this monotone sound of me
trying too hard to read like a poet covers up the
redneck in my voice.

I was once told that I say the number *nine* wrong

by a girl from Indiana. We spent the rest of
vacation correcting each other's accents on
a towel in the sand. And maybe you don't
understand, but I was always one to be in
love with lust.

Even so, as I lay here sprawled out, bare-naked,
in front of you, again… my chest and stomach
hair gone, so that in the proper shadows of light,
you can just make out the four-pack that I've
been working so hard on for the last two months.

And if I keep it flexed just right, perhaps, you
won't notice the case of Busch Light that I
crushed around the fire with the guys last night.

Aspiring Writer

We say it with such conviction
that it's almost convincing to
wide-eyed listeners of our own
hopes and dreams.

But, what makes a writer a writer?

Surely, it's not just scribbles of
nouns, verbs, and adjectives from
a new pen that came in a pack of
ten.

No, writing *must* be loyalty.

To aspire from the valleys and
rivers of yesterday's garbage; to
pull yourself out of that white water
pooling of wadded up mistakes, and
climb back up that falling crystal to
where the sun shines still, to boldly
mark that you are *here;*

and then shout out your voice so
clear that it echoes from rock to
tumbling rock, from cliff to glaring
cliff; I am Writer! I am Writer!

Autumn in Her Arms

We sat under jewels in a purpled sky;
the hours passing like strokes through
her autumn hair. Our conversations deep,
drowning in her hazel eyes; *does love
exist? Or are we conditioned to believe
that it's real? Well, what about aliens? Or
Professor Wilson's hair?* Our laughter
flicking on red-eyed neighbor's porch lights.

But if we had a care in the world, we didn't
show it. Instead, she lit another cigarette
from half a pack left, and I watched as she
burned that cherry down, sending smoke
signals into the street lamped night. I hated it,
but I couldn't help it. Her charcoaled kisses
and embered lips brought me and the night
to flames.

Jacob Paul Patchen

Sweet Red

Mogen David Blackberry, in a Wal-Mart glass;
four-dollar wine staining the last glass still standing
from the frail set.

I fill it high, for me. And you lift your left nostril, the
skeptical one, the cute one… if nostrils can be
cute.

Another half a glass in and you'll find me kissing
it. But for now, I smirk at your high dollar tongue,
and thanks to your merlot, it's slightly more red
than it was an hour ago.

And mine is purple, to match my teeth and lips;
as sweet as the berries on the label; I somehow
convince you that it's amazing.

And you, being amazing too, question my palate
with a cute, crinkled nose.

But I'm not ashamed of my sweet tooth, the
bluish red one, which so often craves your lips,
your thighs, and everything in between. It obviously
knows it's sugar.

OF LOVE AND WAR

You take the glass from my raised arm-and-brow
offering. Swirling that candy to the edges, you
inspect it, analyzing it, pausing one last time before
you pull it up for a squinting and doubtful
sniff.

And I can't help but notice your dramatically
raised pinky as you suck in that sweet sip…
just to spit it back out.

Jacob Paul Patchen

Mixed Signals and Mixed Drinks

Nine-dollar half glasses of wine.

Back home, that'd be a bottle
and some chocolates.

I'm in my good jeans and flannel;
no holes or mud stains; in a room
full of table manners, pressed khakis
and ties.

I'd feel out of place if you'd ever
stopped looking at me, if you ever quit
that contagious smile and rolled eyes
that we share from table two's fake laughter,
as we pile stirring straws next to this lit,
three candle set, center piece.

I order up another captain 'n coke
from a better dressed waiter, you take a
vodka and tonic, just a splash, and
with a small straw.

I watch as your exaggerated lips suck up
the last sip and all of my attention
in that zebra skirt that you swear
is just from Kohl's.

OF LOVE AND WAR

And if we didn't pause to laugh at these banquet strangers, I'd forget that we are not alone; and that we

are not together, either.

Tinder Me

Who are we,
the desperate and despaired?
Downloading an App to our Androids
and OtterBoxed iPhones –
     blurry-eyed
in the search for love.

Love.

Do we even know what that is?
Is that even *a thing* anymore?

Maybe I'm just doing it all wrong,
hoping for something more while
swiping a quick *no thanks* to those
     duckface selfies,

And instead,
pausing for your smile-with-me-smile,
evaluating
your hold-my-hand blue eyes
     soft for the fall and open.

Drunk, again. I stumble right in,

OF LOVE AND WAR

Click to your profile and re-read two times:
"must make me laugh often, buy me tacos,
    cuddle
and love all dogs"

Hell, she might as well have said
that his name must be *Jacob*.

I swipe a confident right.
And imagine

our messy taco Tuesday nights,
lazily wrapped
in a fuzzy blanket on a dog-haired couch,
cracking up to my silly stupidity while
I stroke my fingers through your hair.

    And I wait.

But your vibrations never come.

Jacob Paul Patchen

Shopping Wal-Mart

My dear stimulating stranger
with sunshine hair,

what led us here,

fast paced and rancid,

to the same aisle
of memory foam
pillows

and heavy down
comforters;

where we sidestepped
in unison

like two slow dancers
in the ballroom lights
flickering abuzz,

above us

in aisle four?

Are we merely sleepwalkers,
in the tide of nightmare zombies?

Or is it meant

that we should put to test
the comfort

of these thousand thread count sheets?

Jacob Paul Patchen

Warm by the Moonlight

She wore the moonlight
like her favorite fleece blanket,
familiar and warm,
sitting there in the darkness
of a summer's porch night
confessing her divorce tragedies
to the stars and me;
waiting for something new to
wish upon
for something brighter
to light her way.

She deserved the morning sun,

and I was willing to give it to her.

OF LOVE AND WAR

She Curses in the Morning

She curses in the morning;

tripping over a pile of dirty
clothes in the blacked out
darkness from a set of Big
Lots curtains,

calling my life chaos with her
hair matted to one side, sticking
up on the other, in nothing but
a wrinkled shirt, inside out and
backwards, from her own disorder.

I just smile, my proud eyes
adjusting to her darling form
haloed by the bathroom light,
laughing at her grumpy face
staggering towards the bed and
me.

But she smacks my beer gut as
she slides into bed and over onto
her side, scolding me with a cold
shoulder.

And if I told her how cute I think
she is, I'm certain that I'd never see
another beautiful morning.

Dessert

I love you.

And I haven't said
it in such a long time
that I have forgotten
how chewy
the words can be,

sticking to the
roof of my mouth
like dark chocolate,

such a delicate dessert,
sweet on the sides of
my tongue
where I hold them for
a moment,

sucking in the sugars,
hoping
that this lasts through
dinner;

So then I can
open you up
and enjoy you
like a gold Govida truffle.

Winter Coming

It's the first cold rain
on the second day of September.

There is a pumpkin spice latte
steam hanging in the trees, on the leaves,
and rolling up my Facebook newsfeed.

The glare of a grey sky on the
wet blacktop, interrupted by the blur
of grocery shoppers speeding into
town.

I watch puffy breasted robins mixed
in with speckled starlings, bobbing at
the soggy green and brown-patched yard.

I exhale rudely and shake my head in disgust
to the one hopping in front, who cocks his
head, inflates and shakes beads of fall from
his ruffled hazelnut belly.

And I pat mine, calming the growing growl,
breathing in the spicy tang of fresh
stovetop chili, which encourages
a large cheesy bowl,
and a full day of football couch coaching.

Jacob Paul Patchen

I Still Sleep with This Gun

I still sleep with this gun.

Reaching out to adjust it on
this nightstand, the rear sight's
green glowing eyes
      meeting mine,

that's how I like it,
      intimate and piercing,
looking into the shaded corners
of this cracked shell of reason;
      where ambushing nightmares
of a whistling mortar's thunder
still wait in the black haze
of my room;

I clear them out with a mounted
tactical light.
      The shaking hiss of my breath
blowing truth
      against these walls.

With it in my hand,
     I stand a chance, its weight grounding my conscience, pulling me back from shaded places.

It is rough, heavy, and cold.

It is perfect and comfortable.

About the Author

Jacob Paul Patchen was born and raised outside of Byesville, Ohio where he spent his youth tormenting babysitters and hiding in trees. Patchen earns his inspiration through experience, where he writes abundantly about love, war, sex, family and drinking. Jacob is a poet, an author, blogger and combat veteran. He debuted with his 5 star rated book, *Life Lessons from Grandpa and His Chicken Coop: A Playful Journey Through Some Serious Sh*t* (2015) and *Talking S.H.I.T.* (Social, Humorous, and Inspirational Thoughts) (2017). Patchen is published in several literary journals, including *New Millennium Writings, Into the Void Magazine, The Deadly Writers Patrol,* and *Lost Lake Folk Opera Magazine.* He has also been selected as a finalist in many poetry competitions.

Acknowledgments

My strength comes from those closest to me, who allowed me to read to them my most sacred confessionals, which were at times, both haunting and disturbing; and ultimately it comes from those who refused to believe in me. Thank you to my loving, supportive, and lying family, who always claimed that my poetry was perfect. Thank you friends, fans, and ex-lovers for the disbelief, the support, and deepest of inspirations.

"To be the Westward Sky at Sunset" and "We Sleep with Mice and Vipers" were first published in *GFT Presents: One in Four*.

"Fireflies on the City" was first published online by GFT Press in their *Ground Fresh Thursdays* section.

"Dying in the Light" was first published by *Veterans Writing Project: O-Dark-Thirty*.

"Shadows in the Lamplight" was first published online by *The American Journal of Poetry*.

"Death Letter" was first published by *Military Experience & the Arts* journal: As You Were.

"Broken" was first published in *GNU Journal*.

"Mortar Us," "The Pistol on my Nightstand," and "On Seeing the Ginger from across the Bar and Hoping that She's Easy" were first published in *Lost Lake Folk Opera Literary Magazine*.

"Lime Trees in Paradise," "Throwing Rocks at the Shitter and Me," and "Of Love and War" were first published by *The Deadly Writers Patrol*.

"Dog Barking at 4 a.m. on a Wednesday Morning" was selected as a finalist in the 43rd New Millennium Awards for Poetry and published by *New Millennium Writings*.

"How to Hold Your Head Up" was first published by *Edify Fiction Magazine*.

"To Feel Alive" was first published by *Writing Knights*.

"I'd Love to Lay You Down" was first published by *Into The Void* magazine, Issue 6.

"Unshakable She," "Ground Watcher," and "Letting Go" first appeared in *Foliate Oak Literary Magazine* December issue 2017.

"Dying at Work" was first published by *The Veterans Writing Project* in The Review 2018.